Red Top Farm
Fond Memories

Martha Newman

Our Farm

by my father Laurence P. Melton

Our farm, to me, is not just land
Where bare, unpainted buildings stand;
To me, our farm is nothing less
Than all created loveliness.

> Our farm is not where I must soil
> Tired hands in endless, dreary toil;
> But where through seed and swelling pod,
> I learn to walk and talk with God.

Our farm to me is not a place
Outmoded by a modern race;
Instead it's where I just see less
Of evil, greed and selfishness.

> Our farm's not lonely, for all day
> All Nature is at work and play;
> And here, when age comes, free from fears
> I hope to live long, joyous years.

Our farm's a haven, here dwells rest,
Security and happiness.
Whate're befalls the world outside,
Here faith and hope and live, abide.

> Sweet mystery of death and life,
> Unsolved by man's eternal strife
> To guess the truth by test or creed
> While blinded by his lusts and greed.

Should'st Thou, O God, my soul elate,
From death—and birth—to incarnate
A life refreshed from evil's harm,
I pray Thee take me to our farm.

> And so our farm is not just land
> Where bare, unpainted buildings stand;
> To me, our farm is nothing less
> Than all God's hoarded loveliness.

With A. D. "Cat," Kent and Kay
They make the farm a place to say—
Hi, folks—you're welcome sure;
Enjoy God's air—it is fresh and pure.

*I*n today's world, rural America is an anomaly. Anyone who has not had the occasion to spend time there is missing out. Luckily, I had parents who were born on a farm and in later years, they wanted to experience it again. If it wasn't for them, I would have missed the wonderful rural experience.

—Martha

Chapter 1

The dirt road kicked up dust behind us like fog. We had to slow down to cross ditches made by the last rain—not knowing how long ago the rain had fallen. My family bounced along, which included my father Laurence, my mother, Fanny, my sister, Peggy, and me—Martha.

The road was named Rat Road. I didn't want to know why it had that name, but as we drove along it, I saw out the back seat window, pastures filled with over grown weeds.

As we approached the turn-in, my father called out with much excitement: "We're here!"

There before us stood a dilapdated, ancient farmhouse amid waist-high grass and weeds. Peggy and I looked at each other, unable to believe that our Sunday "mystery drive" had ended here.

"Be careful on the steps and the porch," my mother warned. "It's a little broken down."

That was definitely an understatement. Inside the house was no better. The house had been abandoned for many years and I vividly remember the smell-the old wood mixed with a distinctive skunk odor. I held my nose as we walked through the four rooms.

My parents' smiles beamed. "It's ours!" my father exclaimed.

Indeed, I thought; but why? I wondered. Both my parents had grown up on farms and left as soon as they could get jobs in the big city. After World War I, my father left the family farm in Decater, Texas to move to Fort Worth and then on to Dallas to open a printing business. My mother moved from her family farm (she was one of seven siblings) in Lancaster, Texas to Fort Worth and she and her sisters got jobs as telephone operators, also known as "hello girls."

Done with the farm life, both my parents became what they called "citified." Through the years, especially when we lived in far west Oak Cliff on Brooklyndell Street, we had a garden. During the war years of the 1940s our garden grew and almost sustained all of our food needs. Even with that dependence on the garden during World War II, I never imagined that they would return to farming or ranching at the level this farm represented.

Several summers, when I was young, I went to Jane, Missouri to stay with my Great Aunt Nell and Uncle Port. They lived on a chicken farm in the back woods. My father was born in Jane and everyone loved it when we came to visit. I did not like some of the country inconveniences. There was an outhouse and heavy quilts on the bed for the chilly evenings, which I slept under, still shivering. I had never been to such a deep, dark place as in those woods. When you looked out the window it was solid black. However, there were things that I loved, such as floating in inner tubes down the creek that flowed rapidly by my aunt and uncle's house. I also enjoyed the nights when the neighbors went to an empty barn and danced to Uncle Port's fiddle playing. I learned to drive on those back roads. That was my only experience with farm life until Red Top Farm was bought.

The parcel of land was approximately 180 acres with a creek called Tickey Creek that ran through it. It had a dilapidated house, two ponds, a barn, a chicken coop and a small house on a hilltop. "That will be the tenant house and the garden will be up there," my mother told us. She was a little less exuberant than my father, but I was still amazed as she continued with her plans.

"We'll have chickens and fresh eggs and we'll raise cantaloupes…" Peggy and I could not believe our ears. It was 1947 and I was still in high school; my older sister, Peggy, had graduated and was working at the State Fair. We soon learned that the farm was a dream that our parents had shared for a long time—and over time we came to appreciate that it was one of the best investments they ever made for our family. But it took time…

On Thursday afternoons my father and mother would pack the station wagon up to the ceiling and head north. The farm was located east of McKinney and south of the small community of Princeton. The closest settlement was Culleoka, which was only a tiny grocery store run by Homer and Lou Judd. Lou would say of the couple, [we're as] "Old as the hills."

The two closest neighbors were the Jacksons, namely Ross, age sixty and his mother. They planted acres and acres of corn and brought bushels across the road to us. Neither of the Jacksons had ever been to Dallas. "Why, it's not peaceful there," Mrs. Jackson proclaimed.

My father began his time there improving the house. He wanted to modernize it. The house had a large kitchen (which got new appliances), but the best feature were the two screened-in porches that were built (a north porch and a south porch). The south porch became a sleeping porch with army cots lined up side-by-side. The existing front porch was repaired and white rocking chairs were placed on it that faced Rat Road. My parents liked to sit on the front porch and watch the "traffic," although no more than three cars a day passed by. It wasn't long before morning glories were climbing the porch pillars.

A brick fireplace was built in the living room. It was my father's pride and joy. He put his mother's clock, her oil lantern and a huge

brass longhorn head purchased at the State Fair by a friend on the mantle.

Linoleum was put down on all the floors, except for the living room. We thought the new indoor/outdoor carpeting made it oh so modern. Some new and secondhand ranch/farm furniture was added along with some family antiques.

These include my maternal grandmother's wicker rocking chair, large oval-framed pictures of grand and great-grand parents, and a coffee table carved with a cattle drive and topped with glass. Other items included antique plates and a large pitcher painted with roses, which had been in my grandmother's house for as long as I remember. In a place of prominence sat the old pump organ that had belonged to my Aunt Margarite. I remember when she had it in her house, we all stood around and sang as she played, "Beer Barrel Polka." The bedrooms were simply furnished and the two bathrooms had new (modern) sliding glass doors around the tub, which was in all the latest home magazines.

There was one room that was strictly my father's. This was where he kept his fishing and hunting gear, all of his farm clothes, his decoys, and most fascinating of all—his CB radio set. My father spent his "resting time" talking to other CB enthusiasts, chatting like people do now on the Internet or over Twitter. I remember hearing: "Come in," "What's your handle," as he spoke into a microphone. I wish I could remember his handled, but there is no one around any more to ask. CB stands for Citizen Band. It was a system of short distant communication between individuals on a selected channel. It was also referred to as a ham radio. An operator's license was only twenty dollars, but the equipment for a ham radio was expensive. We had a very tall antenna beside the house and the radio took over the top of a big desk. Only one person could transmit at a time; others had to listen until a channel was available.

The Federal Communication Commission was formed in 1934 and this was the body that in 1945 permitted average citizens, families and small businesses to have particular channels to communicate. Over the decades CB clubs were formed and a CB language developed. It became a national craze. My father especially liked to talk to truck drivers about where they were and where they were headed, the weather and a variety of topics. When Lunk (the nickname his grandchildren came up with and taken up by almost everyone else) was in his CB room and someone was looking for him, someone would inevitably start singing the song "Convoy," which was a popular hit about CBs in the 1970s.

My father had other hobbies such as painting horses with paint by number kits which were popular in the 1950s and 60s. I wish I had kept some of those paintings.

The farm progressed year after year into a habitable, even comfortable place. A white rail fence encircled the large yard. So many family members pitched in to help paint. Fanny would make gallons of iced tea and gallons of homemade ice cream for the helpers. Not only was the house repaired and painted, a carport, a storage shed and a detached covered patio were built. The original wood stove from he kitchen was moved there. The wood stove was a favorite place to cook delicious breakfasts. Tables, lounge chairs and flowers (cannas) were planted around the border. That is where we ate most of our meals all summer long.

In fact, everyone stayed in the yard most of the time. A swing was stretched from the large oak tree and an old flat wagon was put in the yard to use as a table, or even as a bed. My uncle Hank often slept there.

Chapter 2

Tickey Creek was dry in the summer. A hot, dry wind would make enormous cracks in the creek bed—big enough for your foot to go through. But in the spring, the creek flowed enough to wade and it fed into a small pond that had some small fish in it. We would take cokes and peanut butter on crackers and sit by the pond and fish.

Usually we had to throw our catch back because of how small they were. It only took a couple of years and Red Top was ready to be an actual farm again. The pastures were plowed and planted with oats and alfalfa. A new barn was built, as was a large chicken house, a corral, a foaling pen and loafing pens dotted the land. Two dozen white-faced cattle were grazing on the hilltop. Eventually, they were replaced by black Angus. We got Landrace hogs (the ones with two extra ribs) a small pony name Stormy, and a collie named Happy joined the menagerie.

Two new lakes were dug and stocked with fish. My father purchased an adjoining fifty acres. The largest lake had a wooden pier where we took our fishing gear and settled in lounge chairs that were left on the bank. All afternoon (and some nights) fish were caught, cleaned and fried for dinner. Lanterns were lit at night, but I was terrified by the snakes that swam toward the light; so I usually stayed behind on the night fishing expeditions. I didn't like rabbit hunting at night either and was content playing cards with my mother on the screened-in porch.

Once the farm was made comfortable, friends and family came to enjoy respite from city life. On weekends, we would have a stream of visitors. My parents relished giving directions: "Go to Culleoka, cross Tickey Creek, turn left on Rat Road, and look for the red roofs."

My Aunt Bonnye and Uncle Hank came every weekend. My aunt was mourning the loss of her only son and the farm proved to be a wonderful place to help her heal. Hank loved the farm, too. He had his pack of Busch beer and he would plug in his radio on the patio so he could listen to the University of Texas

football games. They never missed the Austin games and always had a bit of burnt orange on during the radiocasts. Bonnye and my mother, Fanny, worked hard together in the garden. They grew cantaloupes (as my mother had predicted) and also every other vegetable you can name.

They reconstructed the peach orchard, and the two of them by themselves built a wire fence to keep out the rabbits and other wildlife. I can still conjure up the sound of Bonnye and Fanny's laughter and conversation as they worked. There was always quite a commotion whenever the chickens got into the garden. Both family members and visitors would rush up the hilltop to shoo the intruders back to their roost. Bonnye was also a good upholsterer and took any old chair or sofa and made it like new. She took charge of repairing the outdoor furniture, as well. She did this task on the bed of the outdoor wagon while others stood around to comment.

My father, Laurence, was in his element managing the farm. On Thursdays, the stop at Sears to order new equipment was a must. The cattle and horse auctions in McKinney were a welcome Saturday outing for Peggy and him. My cousins, Nancy and Jack, were there most weekends. All through their childhood and teenage years they were regulars at the farm. Other family members would come out for the day on a Saturday or Sunday. My parents entertained business associates at large picnics.

Every year on opening day of dove season, my father hosted a day-long shoot for about thirty friends. It was well organize with trucks taking the hunters to their stands in fields of swaying sunflower blossoms. All day long we heard the "Pow! Pow! Pow!" of the shotguns. When the hunters returned, they were met

14

with large coolers of beer. While George, one of my father's very loyal employees at his printing company, cleaned the birds and packed some in ice for each hunter to take, Fanny and Bonnye would be frying other doves in huge skillets for our dinner. Peggy, Nancy, Jack and I were in charge of setting the long tables set up in the yard with gingham cloths for the annual "Hunt Dinner." Other feasts included bar-b-ques for the Scout Masters of Circle 10. Every year, each event grew larger, but my father thought they were grand.

One weekend when I was home from college, the farm proved to be a scene of a dramatic occasion. My fiancée came to ask my father for my hand in marriage. They walked the fence line and talked while my mother and I looked from the back porch and tried to understand what was being said. The men returned without smiles or words of encouragement. My father recommended that we wait until we were more certain of the military's plan for my intended. There were lots of tears that day (mostly on my part), but it worked out well the next year. We were married and the farm visits included one more family member.

Another time my college roommate and her boyfriend (who lived in nearby Greenville) came to visit us at the farm. She found an engagement ring at her place setting at Sunday dinner. That engagement was met with applause and hugs all around.

Years later, after marriage and when my immediate family increased to five, the farm took on a new dimension for me. As a four-year-old, my daughter Linda was kept busy swinging, watch-

ing the farm animals and riding the pony while her infant twin sisters slept in two of the eight cozy cribs on the porch and in the house. They went from cribs to playpens outdoors and as they grew, they spent long periods of time in the two-seater glider. They never tired of swinging back and forth facing each other.

As the girls got older, they explored the farm. Linda would go to the hilltop to gather eggs, work in the garden with Fanny, and just "be gone" within the limits of the farm. The twins, Laura and Robin, were content to stay closer, taking walks with others or playing in the yard. The girls could go across the small bridge that Lunk built across a gully north of the house. The farm represented freedom and provided slow, relaxed days that we all welcomed.

The farm was filled with wonder for our visitors and family. One time when we still had pigs, my father woke all of us up at midnight. Our friends and their four-year-old and five-year-old children, Linda and a few others piled into the jeep and rushed to the barn. We watched twelve piglets enter into the world. It was an amazing sight for me, and I'm sure for the others, too. I also learned that pigs really do squeal "oink, oink, oink."

Mud was just an inconvenience to us at the farm. We had rubber boots for everyone who needed them, which was often. After it rained we would tramp around the yard in a gooey mess. The children loved it!

Whenever a dark cloud appeared in the sky or a clap of thunder was heard, everyone would scatter, run to their cars and move them to the pavement a mile down Rat Road. Then they had to walk back, hoping not to get caught in the rain. Sometimes they would draw straws to find "volunteers" to move the vehicles. Many a time the volunteers would come back soaked, which everyone thought was funny. Eventually Lunk bought a jeep and would bring the volunteers back.

In fact, almost every calamity seemed funny. For example, once day some of our neighbors' cows got out and were in our pasture, which happened from time to time. The crowd gathered at Red Top went out to herd them home. We finally got them to the road and they began to run. We tried to guide them back to their own pasture but they kept going and we couldn't keep up. Someone got in the jeep and got the herd turned around. Then the cows were chasing us like the bulls in Spain. The rancher and his sons finally arrived and took over the situation. We laughed about that for years.

Another time, a stranger was spotted in the lower pasture. We all watched from the house, wondering who he was: A trespasser? A hunter? A fugitive? Some of the men went to investigate and came back laughing. It was a ten-year-old boy on his way to a fishing hole.

Chapter 3

Red Top Farm was isolated. It had one of only two houses on the dirt road, but we always felt secure. Nevertheless, a shotgun was always handy. There were just so many people there on most days that no one would dare intrude.

A disaster of another kind happened one spring. The dam of the larger lake broke and flooded and washed out the road. We didn't think it was a problem because there was access at the other end. Then that part of the road washed out. We were stranded. It was the only time that happened, but it turned into a fun weekend for all of us. We cooked chili and beans and watched The Rifleman, Have Gun Will Travel (Lunk's favorite), and The Jack Benny Show. Some of us played gin rummy or solitaire. For more than two days, which included a Monday, we could not get down the road or even leave the house. Finally someone volunteered to take the jeep to see if they could get to the cars parked on the pavement. Much to our disappointment, they were accessible, so we made our way from the relaxation of the farm to the demands of the city. After the flooding experience, my father pestered the commissioners to gravel Rat Road.

There was a storm cellar in the yard. It was covered with earth and grass but had a metal door. Steps led down to an earthen room about four by six feet. I was not very brave, but did dare to enter that cellar, but others did not mind going down there on any threatening cloud. The occasion that sent me down there was an intense storm, which roared through one morning, taking down telephone poles and fences. Thankfully, we only had to stay down in the cellar a few minutes. That was enough for me, so when storms approached I decided it was best to take my chances in the house.

The cellar was like a mini ramp and several of us thought it was fun to ride the motor scooter that some visitor brought to the farm one weekend. Then Peggy tipped it over when she was going over the cellar and fell off and

A trend at the time was for homeowners to wallpaper the ceilings in their homes. So naturally, we decided to paper the bedroom and bathroom ceilings in pretty flowered paper. To do the work we took the wallpaper roll and put it on the large round dining table, lathering on the paste that we had mixed up in a pan. We used wide bristled brushes. Together, on ladders, we held the strips of wet paper and placed them on the ceilings.

Everyone who was there that weekend helped us and we had lunch outdoors. Fanny fixed her standard rashers of bacon and scrambled eggs. We had fresh cantaloupes and tomatoes from the garden. There was also cream gravy and biscuits. Fanny liked to put gravy on her cantaloupe and when she did, we all rolled our eyes.

broke her leg. That ended that amusement. I think it was her carelessness rather than the inherent danger of the cellar because my mother and father rode over the cellar on the riding lawnmower many times without incident.

Whenever we were at the farm our time was usually spent out of doors, especially if the weather was good. On Saturdays and Sundays, a small airport just two or three miles away gave skydiving lessons. We would sit in lawn chairs and watch the skydivers jumped from the low-flying planes. The white parachutes would often glide down close by and one time one of them dropped down just across the road. My father took the skydiver back to the airport in the jeep. One time was terrifying when we were watching the sky one afternoon and one of the parachutes did not open. We all caught our breath. We heard the sirens. No one spoke of it and after that day, we never watched the skydivers again.

After lunch we went back and finished the ceiling wallpapering project. It was hard work and we all fell into our beds that night. During the night as the paste dried, many of the pieces wouldn't hold and began to drop. At three o'clock in the morning we found ourselves putting the paper back on the original rolls. We didn't try it again. My mother's comment was, "Fun while it lasted!"

My father bought an army jeep to the farm. It was army green and open on all sides. Six passengers could fit in it—or seven if they hung on tight enough. In the late evening, he would summon everyone to load up into the jeep to "make the circle," stopping at the Judd's for popsicles or nutty buddies and then down across Tickey Creek bridge and Rat Road back to Red Top. The "circle" became something of a tradition.

None of us believed it would work, but when my father told us a man was coming that afternoon to find water for a well with a "water witch." He said it with such conviction that we all said, "well maybe."

We watched as an old man stepped out of his pickup with nothing but a long-forked stick. My father told us he was someone who could find underground water and many of the neighbors had convinced him that it was possible.

"It's called a divining rod," the old man said. "Not everyone can do it, you know. It works for some folks. I've found at least 50 wells in all these 20 years. It's a gift, but it comes in spurts, I never know when I will find water. I use a freshly cut peach tree twig."

We were fascinated.

He held the sprig palms down, thumbs up. "If the branch gets over a good water source it will bend over. There's a streak of water under the ground. Right here. If I take one step, the twig won't move. You have to be right over water. See look at it. I don't know why it works, but I have the gift."

My father marked the spot and then asked what he owed the "douser."

"Nothing! I can't charge for my water witching because if I do, the gift will disappear." With that, he shook my father's hand and drove away.

We stood motionless, in awe.

Since I have researched "water witching" and found that there is reference to it in the Bible. Some think it began with Moses (Numbers 20:9-11). There is written in ancient Greek manuscripts of finding water with a forked twig in 1556. Today there are many who use this method all over the world. There are as many as 20 "diviners" in North Carolina.

In the dictionary, a divining rod is "a tool used by one who finds water underground by super natural powers." I also learned that "witch" comes from witch hazel used by early American settlers who used this unusual method.

As far as Red Top Farm and the water witch, a well was dug and there was water, but how much, I am not sure. It was, by all means, the most talked about event at that time.

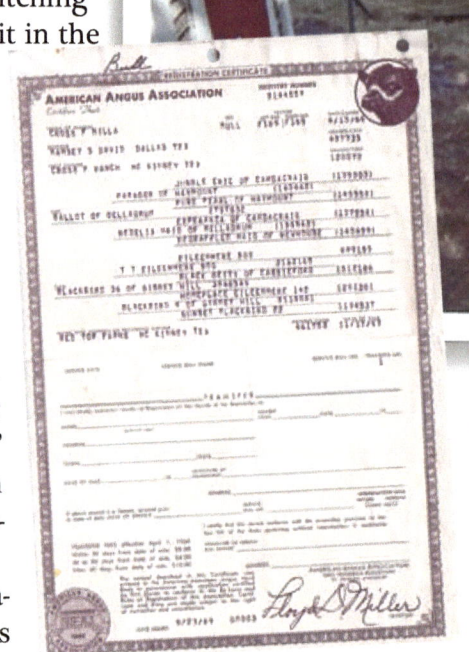

One day, my mother and I were sitting outside chatting about the nice cool breeze, drinking Cokes and eating potato chips. It was one of those dear memories of a moment of complete peacefulness. Suddenly, not six feet in front of us, a huge black snake slithered across the yard. I screamed and jumped into my chair and as quick as I could do that, Fanny, the farm girl that she was, had grabbed the hoe and chopped its head of off. I always marveled at my mother's quick reaction to crisis. Then I remembered the stories she told of how she was the star basketball player on a team that went to the state championship. I could just imagine Fanny making those quick moves on the gym court.

The twins, Robin and Laura, became more excited to go to the farm as they got older and at times they would invite their friends along. Linda also invited friends to come with us or to go with just their grandparents. Linda and her friend, Donna Kay, spent two weeks one summer riding horses and enjoying the outdoors. One day, they were leading their horses back to the barn when Lunk's prize bull came running after them.

They ran as fast as they could and jumped into the watering trough. Drenched, but safe, they came into the house sputtering their narrow escape. Later on Robin and Laura, I recall, also found the watery haven when the bull spotted them in his pasture.

Chapter 4

Hans and Gerta and their two children lived and worked the farm for us for three years. They were from Germany and had been in the United States for a few months when they moved to Red Top. A church in McKinney sponsored their immigration after World War II. Hans, like my father, was a veteran who had been in both World Wars.

At first we wondered how the situation would work, my father, a retired American officer and Hans a retired German soldier, but we need not have worried. The two of them, remarkably, put their experiences behind them and found a common thread in sharing farm work and caring for the animals. There was a language barrier, but my father was a gregarious man who talked with his hands and often his whole body—so did Hans. We were all amused to see them sitting under a tree in animated conversation.

"What are they talking about?" someone would ask.

"Who can tell?" another would answer.

Most of the time it would be about cattle or some equipment. I think at times that they must have talked about wartime. But my father never discussed his battlefield experiences. After about a year, Gerta was expecting a baby and when she went into labor, our whole family, plus one guest, went to the hospital in McKinney in the middle of the night. That seems very strange to me now. "Why did we all go?" The baby boy weighed eleven pounds and they named him Frederick.

It seemed so sudden to us when Hans and Gerta decided to take another job the church found for them on a large produce farm in California. Having them on our farm was a lesson in extreme forgiveness.

There was an ironic twist to Hans and his family being at the farm. 390,000 German prisoners of war were brought to Canada and the United States in 1945. A prison camp had been constructed in Princeton, less than ten miles from Red Top. It

was a row of wooden dormitories surrounded by a tall barbed wire fence and four watchtowers. My father said guards on horseback patrolled the outskirts.

By the time my father purchased the farm, the prisoners had been sent back to Germany, but the camp stayed intact for years. It could be seen from the highway and we took a closer look at it several times.

As I think back on it, I'm amazed that there was Hans, a free German ex-soldier, living a short distance from where a thousand or more of his countrymen had been imprisoned. A strange quirk of history.

The Adcocks and their two children stayed the longest of any tenant. They had been born in Culleoka and knew everyone within miles and miles. They had a life of their own, but sometimes they shared dinner or conversation in the yard. Their children, Kay and Kent, became friends and playmates to my daughters and their cousins. A.D. with his big Stetson hat and brass belt buckle and his country ways had the look of a real cowboy. Catherine was a consummate farmwoman and could do anything around the farm. A. D.'s particular fondness was for the horses. Catherine's was for cooking chicken and homemade dumplings. They left to move into McKinney. After that, my father depended on day workers. The hilltop tenant house stood vacant.

At times, there were some famous people that visited Red Top Farm. Audie Murphy, the most decorated soldier of World War II was born and raised in Farmersville, a few miles from Culleoka. Once he came to the farm and he and my father had lunch in the yard and talked through the afternoon. "A fine soldier and young man," my father told us. I suppose they shared army stories.

Another time, Admiral Chester Nimitz, the commander of the Pacific forces during WWII and also a fellow Texan, drove up to the farm with a driver and an aide. He drank endless cups of coffee in the house by the fire. That visit was a highlight of my father's many different conversations with folks for weeks. The admiral gave him a signed photograph of the signing of the Japanese surrender, which I still have.

Although not as famous, I was impressed when Guinn "Big Boy" Williams spent Sunday with us. He and my father had been childhood friends in Decater and had kept in touch with letters for all those years since. Big Boy" Williams had become a very big supporting actor in many westerns. And he was big! I thought it would be impossible for him to fit through the door. However, I never met a more charming and happy man. He and Laurence laughed uproariously during that visit.

"Ask him about Roy Rogers," I pleaded. But if he did, he never said. My father was exactly the same whether he with a well-known man or a stranger. That was one of his most endearing qualities.

Hildegard was the name my mother gave to the ghost who lived in the little white house by the big lake. My father would suggest a walk at night to see the moonlight over the water or some other excuse to get everyone to walk down the road to the drive up to the house and the lake. He would carry a large flashlight to lead the way. It was scary just to be out of the yard at night anyway. There were

so many night sounds in the country, rustles in the bushes and shadows among the trees. We always tried to be back to the farmhouse before dark if we went out to the barn.

Those of us who were familiar with the night walks knew what to expect, but first timers at the farm didn't have any idea that Hildegard was about to slam open the front door of the abandoned and run-down house, then step out on the porch, her white robe flowing. Screams and hysterics would follow and the group would race down the road.

My cousins, Jackie and Nancy, remembered that it scared them so much, still they went every time, even if they knew it was Fanny in the sheet. No matter how many times we scared others, we were just as scared. What fun!

Chapter 5

The sleeping porch was perhaps the best for remembering the feeling the farm gave us. The porch was long and narrow with beds lined side-by-side —at one end was a table and chairs and that was where we ate and played cards when the weather turned bad. My mother would sprinkle cold water on the sheets before we climbed into bed in the summertime.

Sleeping on the porch was full of the stillness that comes over everything when the sun goes down. Even in the stillness and silence, there were those scary night sounds that can either lull you to sleep or keep you frozen in your army cot wondering what is making the noise. When the moon was shining bright you might see a creature, most probably a possum, cross the yard. Once an owl landed in the cedar tree next to the porch and woke us up and kept us awake until we talked ourselves back to sleep.

My cousins remember lying in bed and watching lightning bugs and listening to the snoring sleepers. Not everyone wanted to sleep on the porch, but for those of us who did, the night brought a wonderful, peaceful sleep—unless you heard digging sounds or the death cry of a rabbit.

There is a sweetness to waking up in the night after days of dry heat and hearing the rain. You could see stars from the porch and get a glimpse of shadows moving across the moon. In Watie Swanzy's poem, "The Farmer," he writes: "For the sun is already up and has drunk the fresh dew from the flower-cup."

Waking up on the sleeping porch was not so poetic. We were usually awakened by the hot morning sun in our eyes. The jay birds had been awake for a long time and chattered and squawked in the trees.

The kitchen of the farm always had fresh produce gathered in the summer—on the counters and in baskets. The neighbors would bring melon and corn. We would gather okra, carrots, and beans from the garden. Most of the days there would be something cooking on the stove, something fresh out of the garden. There were always beans to be snapped to peas to be shelled.

Breakfast was special. Fanny made what was called "gas house" eggs. I have no idea where the name came from, but they still are a family favorite. A hole was torn out in the middle of a bread slice, the slice was grilled with butter on one side, then turned on the other side and an egg was dropped into the hole, and then carefully turned on the first side and grilled. Bonnye would fry pies, usually peaches from the orchard were the filling. That was her specialty. On lazy afternoons, Peggy and I would make fold-over sandwiches—peanut butter and (homemade) apple butter was my preference while Peggy liked potato chips and mayonnaise. These unique sandwiches reminded us of our childhood.

There was an open window on the porch to the kitchen. Robin remembers fondly to awakening to the smell of bacon frying through the window, the clinking of pans and the soft talking of the early-risers preparing breakfast. The wafts of breakfast cooking, woke us up and we would walk into the yard and breathe the morning perfume: the clear air was clear and fresh as the sun climbed over the trees. In the summer those morning reveries did not last long. The sun's hot rays would quickly bear down and you would look for shade. The farm did not have air conditioning in the first two or three years, and even when it was put in, we stayed out of doors.

In the fall however, the mornings were beautiful. The trees lining Tickey Creek were colored in tan and orange. Fallen leaves would be gathered and spread on the table for a centerpiece.

In the winter, not many visitors would be at the farm, but the family still came to sit by the roaring fire, eat popcorn after we had put on boots and parkas and walked down to the barn in the icy sting of the wind.

The barn was another place that gave the farm a special feel. It has stacks of hay piled to the rafters. Saddles and bridles hung on huge hooks. Shovels, rakes and pitchforks were lined against the wall. The horses were in a corral adjoining and they would neigh until someone brought them a carrot. Cattle grazed in wide fields of bottomland.

Charles Dickens wrote that his dream of a perfect life would be to live on a farm in Switzerland surrounded by cows. However, he did not mention working on a farm. Even with the tranquility, I am not sure of that perfection. Take us for example. In the spring and summer when the clover and tall grasses were in bloom on the hill pasture, which was very pretty, we would sit on the rail fence and watch the hired man plow a field.

Through the years, the large yard at Red Top saw a collection of odd and assorted ornaments. There was a hitching post, a wishing well, antique horse-drawn farm implements, corn-sheller, a plastic fish pond with a little boy fishing statue, plastic turtles, squirrels, rabbits, cement statues of all kinds, a large black kettle planted with zinnias, the before mentioned iron bridge over the gully and old iron pots of all sizes. A windmill caught the wind if there was any. The yard was kept mowed up to the fence line and there were large sprinklers that had to be moved often to keep the lawn green. That was a challenge in summer and we had large patches of brown that bothered my mother immensely. There were also large cracks in the ground. My mother planted lots of moon vines. The blossoms were closed in daylight but were breathtaking at night.

There was always a project in progress. One was a building of a wooden seat encircling the large tree in the center of

the yard. With old scrap planks and a hammer and nails, we all took our turn under the supervision of our leader, Lunk. When it was finished and painted red, it was "sittable" (rustic) at best.

There was a brick walkway from the carport to the house. We all carried bricks and thankfully, there was a farm helper who knew how to place them level. We were all proud of that new walkway. An electric light pole was erected at the entrance of the walk. A stop at the nursery brought two tall evergreen cedar trees. We planted them on each side of the entrance to the new walk. As they grew taller, someone had the idea to tie the tops of the trees together to make an arch. A ladder was brought out and a "volunteer" climbed to the top and tied the ends together. As the years passed they grew into a cedar arch to walk through, which was a source of pride.

As the years passed, our excursions to the farm became a large part of our leisure time. We never knew how many visitors would arrive for the weekend. My immediate family

tried to make it just a family place, but when my sister got married and moved to Oklahoma City, she brought many of her friends to the farm, especially in the fall for the Texas/

OU football game. The farm party became famous, but we did not experience it. We had our party in Dallas for our Texas fans, so we only heard about the celebration at the farm. The nice thing about Red Top is that it could be a perfect gathering place for celebrations as well as a place for solitude.

If you were there with a lot of folks you could always get away from the crowd and sit by the pond all afternoon, watching dragonflies flit about on the surface of the water, walk or stroll the paths beaten down by the cattle or just pull a chair to the far end of the yard and nap. Quite often everyone would drift off to find a quiet place to take a siesta or lie on a cot and listen to the locust. Eventually you couldn't help fall asleep. William Wordsworth wrote about, "Letting the day gather and pass." I suppose it was the same in his day. Those who did not choose to nap sat around in the yard and told stories. Here are some that I remember that intrigued me. Once, during the Bonnye and Clyde rampage through North Texas, my Aunt Bonnye and her husband were traveling in the Texas Panhandle. They stopped at a roadside café and one of the waitresses heard my uncle call my aunt "Bonnye." My aunt was about the right size and hair color, so the waitress called the sheriff and my aunt and uncle were taken to jail. Every lawman wanted to be the one to catch the outlaws. The dime phone call brought my father and Dallas Sheriff "Smoot" Smith running out there to clear the two. Bonnye was horrified, but my father told the story over and over to his own and other people's delight.

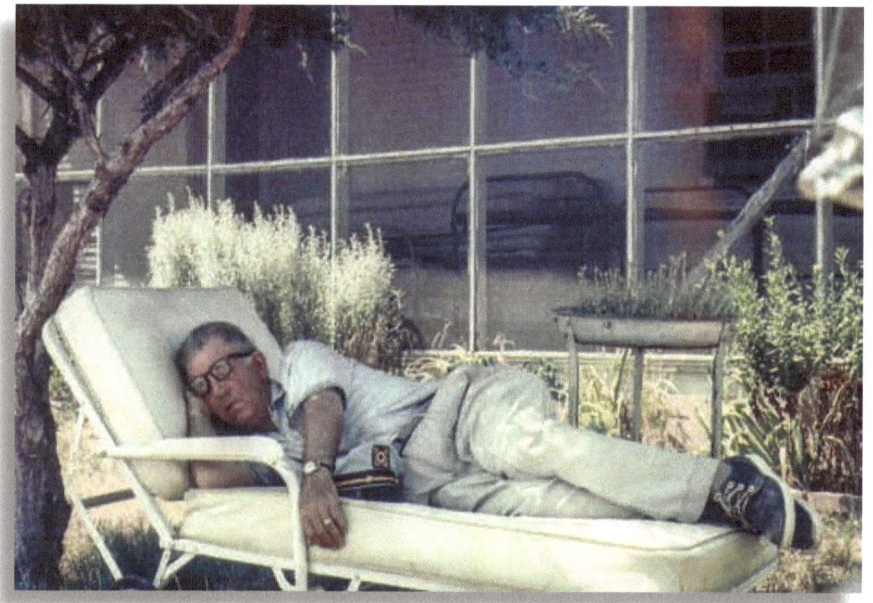

Another story was about my "Big Grandmother" Melton. She was called big because she was larger than my "Little Grandmother," my mother's mother. All of Big Grandmother's relatives were in the egg business in Missouri. Some raised the chickens and others marketed the eggs. To my grandmother's surprise, a carload of relatives came driving up to her house in Fort Worth. My grandmother threw up her hands and exclaimed, "Lordy, Lordy, Lordy. Here's the Missouri folks and not an egg in the house!"

"Whatever happened to Hollis?" was another topic of conversation. Hollis was my older cousin—my Aunt Mabel's middle son. He was always, shall we say, colorful. He visited many times in town and at the farm. He always dressed to

the hilt and drove a nifty sports car or had a driver. He was fun to be around. My family loved him and my father especially enjoyed it when he came to the farm. They would ride out to the pastures in the Jeep. Hollis obviously adored my father and the two of them laughed a lot about old times. One time when he was visiting he told us he had a job in Las Vegas—with Bugsy Siegle! My father was stunned as we all knew that Bugsy was an infamous and feared gangster who was the driving force behind the development of Las Vegas. He was part of the Genovese family that brought the mob to Las Vegas and he turned it into his playground.

After that, the periodic visits by my cousin suddenly stopped. We couldn't understand it. My father tried to find him, and he may have even hired a detective to search for him. Then, years later, I saw the movie Bugsy. In it a hit man makes a mistake and is thrown in front of a train. All I could think was—Hollis!

Intrigued by their conversation from years ago, I decided to do a little research on "A Bledsoe." His real name was Austin and he was born in 1801 and was as tall and large as reported. "Big A," was not only a farmer, but a promoter by spirit. He laid out the town of Lancaster, Texas in 1852 in competition with the town of Pleasant Run, which is now only a tiny bit of land. Lancaster is now a thriving community with a population of 30,000, fifteen miles south of Dallas. He was a force and a county judge in Dallas County during Reconstruction. It is

I remember Bonnye and my mother having the following conversation: "Fanny, do you remember Mama talking about 'Big A' Bledsoe?"

"Who was he? A relative?"

"Yes, I think. I really don't know, except she used to laugh and say when he was born, his father looked at him with pride and said: 'He looks just like a Bledsoe.' He kept that name: 'A Bledsoe' all his life. No one knew any different. He was 6'7" and was 300lbs. Can you imagine?" Bonnye continued, "I saw him lift a mired team out of the mud to help a yoke of oxen."

said he disagreed with Governor E. J. Davis on just about everything while in office. In 1870 he became State Comptroller on the Radical Ticket in 1870. "Honest A" was the name he was called as an elected official. He adhered to the Union during the Civil War, although his son and son-in-law commanded Confederate companies in the South. He died in 1882.

On the lighter side, there were always fish stories. My cousin, Jack, fished with my father many times and they would bring 40 or 50 bass to have for the fish fries that Red Top Farm was famous for throwing. One fish story that my father loved to tell over and over was about his fishing with the Dallas Fire Marshall, Grady Burns. They were fast friends, but one time, when the Marshall fell asleep, my father changed his lure to a different color. The fisherman would pull it out of the water. Grady would wake up, look at it with a frown and then fall back asleep. My father would change the lure again, and again the fisherman would pull it out. After several changes of color, Grady said, "Laurence, I think I had better go back to town and see a doctor."

My father laughed so hard at that story. But then it was his fishing partner's time to play a prank. They loved practical jokes and tried to top each other each time.

The farm work was not like the hard work farmers contend with but for us it was exhausting. At night there was television, a relatively new addition to family life. If we were not too tired from picking peaches and making homemade ice cream, we sat glued to What's My Line, The Jackie Gleason Show, The Ed Sullivan Show and I Love Lucy. Our television was had a small screen, especially compared to today. It was a Dupont and was a simple, pleasant retreat.

It was inevitable that varmints would get into the house at times. It was, after all, a hundred year old house. Although it was remodeled, it was not sealed very well. More than once I had to jump on a chair or table when a field mouse ran across the floor. I'd scream to high heaven until someone came to "do something." Those critters terrified me. One night when I got up to feed the twins, I opened a drawer to get a diaper and found a rat's nest with babies. That caused an indoor hurricane. I will never forget the commotion with people running in circles and with me screaming, and the babies crying. Traps were set after one of these incidents and my mother assured me all of the intruders had been caught. I was never quite sure, though.

My daughter, Laura, remembers the time when she, Fanny and a workman were in the yard and a field mouse ran up Fanny's pant leg. She said, "Excuse me, please" and quickly took off her pants as the workman turned his head. My mother, the farm girl, was once again fearless.

I don't remember when the farm was given the name "Red Top" or when the roofs were reroofed in red shingles. Lunk probably thought of it. The name was on all the registration papers, but the neighbors just called it "The Meltons." When visitors would stop at the Judd's to ask for directions, they would be told to cross the bridge, turn left on Rat Road, and the first house on the left was "The Meltons."

I used to marvel at the endless meals my mother planned and prepared. The preparation and clean up that was involved with so many guests was enormous. And there were so many unexpected guests. I now understand how valuable it is to make others feel comfortable and happy.

There is such satisfaction in giving a successful party and it was a party anytime anyone came to the Red Top Farm.

Chapter 6

There are only a few left who remember the farm.
Each of us who has memories have tried to
pull them together and record them.

My cousins, Nancy and Jack Melton, who spent a great deal of their childhood and teenage years there say it shaped their lives beyond measure. They would spend the night before the weekend with Fanny and Lunk in great anticipation of the ride to the farm in the early morning. Their parents would come to collect them and then spend Sunday dinner with us. The kids never wanted to leave.

Here are a few of their wonderful (and not so wonderful) memories:

Dear Marty,

Thanks for the opportunity to add to a book about Red Top Farm. As you see, some of the remembrances are single incidents that for some reason or another are indelibly etched in my memory. Other things I've written about are an amalgam of reoccurring themes. Nancy and I talked last night, She remembers some things that are different than mine. Use what you can and enjoy reading the rest. It was fun to start thinking about all the wonderful times at the farm. I hadn't thought about some of the things I wrote about for decades. It amuses me that those memories have even survived the passing of time.

—Jack

I guess that everyone has certain words that trigger an overwhelming rush of memories and emotions. For me, two of the strongest are "The Farm." The farm was for me as the Mississippi River was to Mark Twain's Huckleberry Finn. For a city- raised kid, it was a sanctuary with adventure and excitement. It was a place to escape the routine of everyday life and my parents. While I wasn't allowed to run wild, by any means, going to the farm was the equivalent of taking the lid off a popcorn popper.

Sometimes the telephone would ring and Uncle Laurence or Fanny would ask if Nancy or I would like to come to the farm. If it was during the school year, we would excitedly pack our clothes on Thursday night. I would go to Montgomery Wards in Wynnewood to spend my allowance to purchase pellets for my rifle.

More than once, when we told our parents we wanted to go to the farm they would put us on the phone to do the asking. In retrospect, I'm sure it was a prearranged call.

Mother would pick us up from school and take us to the Melton Printing Company where we would wait for Uncle Laurence to load us into his always new station wagon and head for the farm. The wagon was loaded with luggage, food and supplies for whatever new project he was working on.

Sometimes our trip would start from the house in Lakewood where we were delivered by Mother. One time, I spent the night at the Lakewood house before an early morning departure. I was too excited to get much sleep. Every summer we would spend a week or so at the farm. Our parents would join us for a day or two. That usually meant an all night fishing trip on Lake Lavon for Daddy and Uncle Laurence before we all went home. As I got older, the length of our summer stays lengthened. As I look back, I realize that going to the farm was not only a vacation for us, it gave our parents some time alone without Nancy and me—a break from parenting.

Getting to the farm was an adventure in itself. The road out of Dallas headed north on what is now Central Expressway. Sun Drug was on the west side of the road at the edge of civilization. Sometimes we would stop there for a last minute purchase.

The exit off the highway to the farm was to the right of the grain elevator. Uncle Laurence was like a man possessed or at least a man on a mission. When the pavement ended there was a huge cloud of dust behind the station wagon.

A few miles before reaching the farm, we crossed the rickety bridge over Tickey Creek. I remember looking down at the brown water as the planks ogf the bridge made all sorts of scary noises.

Often, our arrival at the farm was at dusk or after dark. Sometimes Fanny arrived earlier in the day. She greeted us with kisses and hugs. After unpacking the car, there was a hot meal waiting for us.

I can still see the layout of the kitchen. There was a cast iron stove on one wall with kindling and wood stacked next to it. On either side of the stove, doors led into the living room. In the center of the room was a large round table that seemingly could seat the entire Melton clan and whoever was there. During the early years, the water wasn't potable, so there was a water dispenser with large inverted bottles of water. I can still hear the glug-glug sound of the large bubbles rising as the water was dispensed. I was intrigued watching my uncle change the heavy bottles without spilling a drop.

There was a bathroom off the kitchen. On the same side of the room, a door led out to a screened porch that was a catch of all the coats, wet clothes, muddy shoes, and small cabinets. A window opening out to the screened porch occupied one wall. Later, a water cooler occupied the window opening. I would stand in front of the cooler on hot summer days after playing outside.

We all slept on the large communal screened porch. At one end were two tall white iron bed for Fanny and Laurence. We were at the opposite of the room in low beds. I remember lying there in the dark, listening to them snoring the night away. As I think about those

nights, I wonder how I slept without so much as a fan,

At the opposite end of the house was another large screened porch. I believe Fanny's sister and her husband, Hank, slept here as well as other guests.

Sleeping on the porch was a part of the magic of our visits. The only thing that separated me from the wilds of my imagination was a thin screen. Sleep did not come easily. I could hear critters scurrying around. I heard cowbells as the cows grazed outside the fence. Crickets chirped and fireflies flitted about the yard. The night was anything but dark. The moon and Milky Way cast deep shadows. I can still see the lightshows provided by summer thunderstorms. There were flashlights beside our beds to find our way to the bathroom should the need arise.

I always awoke before sunrise to see what the day held. Unfortunately, in my younger days, I couldn't get up before the adults. I would just have to lay thre like a kid on Christmas morning.

Breakfast, like all the meals at the farm, was a major production. It seemed like Fanny was always in the kitchen fixing, serving, or cleaning up. Oh how that lady could cook! There were always fresh vegetables from the garden and homemade pies. No one left the table hungry.

After breakfast, the adventures began. I went with Uncle Laurence to check the cows, horses, pigs and chickens. He would talk business with the tenants, veterinarian, or others he had business with. We sometimes took the truck into the fields. It was an old, beat up thing. He also had an old WWII surplus jeep. It had peeling red paint over the olive green. I thought it was really neat because it was a real U.S. Army jeep. I would fantasize about the action it might have seen during the war.

One of my most vivid memories of that jeep involved a skunk. We had taken the jeep down to the store in Culleoka. On the way back, Uncle Laurence hit a skunk, which in turn sprayed the jeep and us. When we arrived at the farmhouse, my clothes were burned rather than taking them home.

Going to the store in Culleoka was an eagerly anticipated trip. I am mot sure what the purpose of those trips were, but Uncle Laurence would buy me a Grapette soda. I would reach into the ice-filled cooler and grab my bottle. There was always a group of men sitting on the front porch whittling, smoking, chewing tobacco and chewing the fat. My uncle would shoot the breeze while I drank my Grapette. At some point, when I was probably 12 or 13, Uncle Laurence told me to put on long pants before going to the store. I understand now that there was a point at which boys were expected to wear "men's" clothing. It was a small important passage into my manhood.

Daddy and Uncle Laurence were especially close as I found out later in life. Laurence was like a father to him. They spent many hours together fishing. While Daddy never verbalized the closeness of their relationship, it was imparted to Nancy and me. Uncle Laurence and Aunt Fanny were one of the constants in our lives. They were aunt and uncle, grandparents, mentors, and authority figures rolled into one.

Below the house there was a typical East Texas creek bottom and a couple of small ponds filled with snakes and turtles. The trees were full of birds. I would ask permission to walk down to the bottom with my pellet gun and a canteen of water. I would spend hours sitting on the banks of those small ponds sharpening my marksmanship. There was some poison ivy, which I learned to identify after some itchy encounters.

The dirt in the bottom was typical Texas. As Daddy said, "you stick to it dry times; it'll stick to you in wet." Occasionally, I would show up at the farm and the bottom would be flooded. One time, I ventured down to the bottom after some recent flooding. The dirt was dry and crusty on top. I ventured onward with the ponds as my goal. I soon found myself ankle deep in black goo. Not wanting to give up, I ventured further. I was soon hopelessly mired and one of my sneakers was sucked off as I tried to turn around. I made it back to the house minus a shoe. Since it was my only pair of shoes, my uncle and I returned to the bottom to retrieve the shoe. I couldn't remember which hole held my shoe and there were a bunch. I had to crawl around on my hands and knees and probe a number of holes until I found my shoe. I was a muddy mess. When I got back to the house, Uncle Laurence hosed me off with the hose in the yard. In retrospect, it was one of those lessons you don't understand until many years later. Come home with both shoes or have a good story to tell.

My adventures at the bottoms usually ended with Uncle Laurence's shrill whistle. I always wanted to whistle like that. You could hear him from incredible distances. I would stick my fingers in my mouth to try to emulate him, but with no results other than a grin from my uncle. In his absence, Fanny would ring the bell located outside the farmhouse, summoning me home.

After eating lunch, we would often lay down on the sleeping porch until the heat of the day had passed. When I was older, I slept in the hammock or a lounge chair under the big tree in the yard.

The time between supper and bedtime was special. The heat of the day had gone. We often made homemade ice cream. I would turn the crank until my arms would give out or the ice cream would be too thick. The adults would sit around laughing and talking. Nancy and I would run around the yard catching fireflies in a Mason jar. We were often given leeway in our normal bedtime schedule. I would sometimes fall asleep in a chair in the yard.

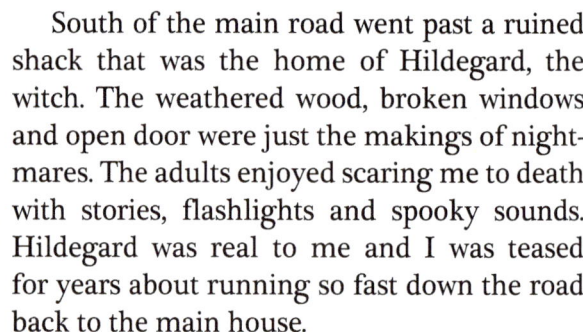

South of the main road went past a ruined shack that was the home of Hildegard, the witch. The weathered wood, broken windows and open door were just the makings of nightmares. The adults enjoyed scaring me to death with stories, flashlights and spooky sounds. Hildegard was real to me and I was teased for years about running so fast down the road back to the main house.

Weekends were always special at the farm. Fanny's sister, Bonnye and her husband, Hank, would show up with food and the ever-present cooler of Busch Bavarian beer. Hank was from a decidedly German family. They wee jovial people and Hank was more jovial with every can. They would laugh and talk for hours. They were so kind to Nancy and me.

Weekends saw the arrival of Martha and Peggy. At some point, Peggy had a red convertible. She was so glamorous with her blond hair and bright red lipstick, which she liberally spread all over us. She would blow in like a Texas thunderstorm. The whole

mood of the place changed. Peggy had a palomino horse and a fancy saddle. We would saddle up the horses and ride all over the farm.

Marty was more reserved than her older sister. She was quieter and had a soft voice. Marty was always so sweet to us. I remember when Marty introduced Stewart, her fiancé, into the family. I was enamored by the military mystique because of Uncle Laurence's service in World War I and II. Stewart was a dashing role model.

Our visits to the farm usually included a trip to Lake Lavon. I think there was more than one boat, but the one I remember most was a Chris Craft. It was all wood—varnished like glass. The chrome and brass was equally gleaming. It seemed so big and noisy. I remember cruising around the lake making a huge wake. I was even allowed to take the helm on occasion. Sometimes, we would fish for hours. I seem to remember Peggy and Marty water skiing.

Laurence was particular about his boat. One time I showed up at the farm without the proper pair of white shoes. Before we could go to the lake, he took me to Princeton to buy me a pair of tennis shoes. We always had to wash and mop the boat before closing it up.

Gun and hunting were also a major activity at Red Top. Uncle Laurence had a .410 pistol that he used to kill starlings and pigeons. I remember the kick that gun had until I got used to firing it.

For years there was a can of fake peanut brittle that was filled with a giant spring covered in cloth. When the top was removed the thing would fly all over the room. Taking a cue from the family, I took pride in asking any unsuspecting guests if they would like some peanut brittle. (That jar belonged to Grandmother Melton who was a joker for many years.)

Our family, most years, joined Fanny and Laurence for Thanksgiving at the farm. On Thanksgiving morning, the three of us went duck hunting at the lake just below the "little white house" down the road (really Hildegard's house). It was my first experience at duck hunting. I just remember how cold and miserable I was.

When I was older, I was allowed to go to the annual September Labor Day dove hunt. It was some affair. I remember Mayor Robert Thornton and other important people of Dallas government. The dove hunt was highly organized. The number one rule was not drink-

One of my visits coincided with the expansion of egg production. There was a shiny new poultry barn and our job was to help assemble the long wire laying cages. Saw horses were set up in the yard and everyone went to work. On my last visit to the farm, not long after Uncle Laurence's death. I went to the chicken yard and paid my respects to the laying cages.

ing until after the hunt. There was no way my dad was going to hunt without a beer while waiting for the birds to fly. At the end of the hunt, there was a huge bar-b-que.

My sister and I loved to fish just like our father and our uncle. We would spend hours fishing in the "big" lake down the road. Sometimes, it was just the two of us. We would crawl through the fence. One time I was going through the fence and I disturbed a nest of yellow jackets. They stung me all over my shoulders, head, and face. I swelled up like a balloon. Fanny put chewing tobacco on the stings to draw out the poison.

Besides poison ivy and yellow jackets, there were chiggers to contend with. At the farm we dusted or socks, shoes, and pants with repellent—Chigger Chaser. When we forgot to dust, our ankles and waists would be covered in bites.

Visits to the farm was not all fun and games. Nancy and I were expected to lend a hand at chores around the place. One of my duties was to bring in firewood and haul out the ashes. I also kept the evaporative cooler filled with water. More than once we were out for long hours harvesting vegetables from the garden. There seemed to be endless amounts of beans to be snapped or corn to be picked and husked.

Uncle Laurence was proud of his black angus herd. I remember a particular bull whose name was "Shorty." He was named for his short legs. That bull was just plain mean. He seemed to get pleasure out of chasing anyone who came near. We would locate Shorty before cutting across the pasture. On more than one occasion we found ourselves running for our lives when we miscalculated the distance or the bull's speed.

As I mentioned before, Peggy had a beautiful palomino. There were other horses around as well. Nancy and I would saddle up a couple of horses and ride the entire place. When I was about twelve, I spent a month at the farm. My uncle had a job for me. It was to help gentle one of his horses. Things were going pretty well until the horse bucked me off into some brambles. I had the wind knocked out of me and a rear full of thorns. I was whimpering. Uncle Laurence told me to get up off my rear and get back on the horse. And I did.

I remember another particular horse. I think it was a paint. It had one eye that was pale blue to the point of being almost white. The horse was spirited and fast. It was fun to ride but with one quirk. You would be plodding along when it would see a can, bottle or some other foreign object. The horse would spook and jump straight up in the air over the object. I would end up on the ground. I soon learned to pay attention to what was ahead.

For years, Laurence grew cotton across the road from Hildegard's house. This was back in the day of braceros going from farm to farm to pick cotton. One time I was asked to pick cotton. They put a sack over my shoulder and I went to work. It didn't last long.

There was a black family around the place for years. I think the man's name was George. They had a pickup and it was always full of kids. There was one boy my age and we would play together.

One year we showed up and there was a new tenant family living on the hilltop. The Adcocks were really nice. They had two kids, Kay and Kent. Kent was a year younger than I was, but we hit if off. His father expected him to work. Chores became fun. The two of us would work together so we could run off and play sooner. I had my .22 pellet gun that when pumped, packed a pretty good wallop at close range. Kent had a Daisy BB rifle. What Kent's lacked in power, he made up for with accuracy. He could outshoot me most of the time. Kent didn't have much spending money so I tried to bring BBs for his gun when I came to the farm. Kent was a perfect companion for my Tom Sawyer adventures. We roamed the place on foot and horseback. His mother would let Kent spend the night with me at the house .

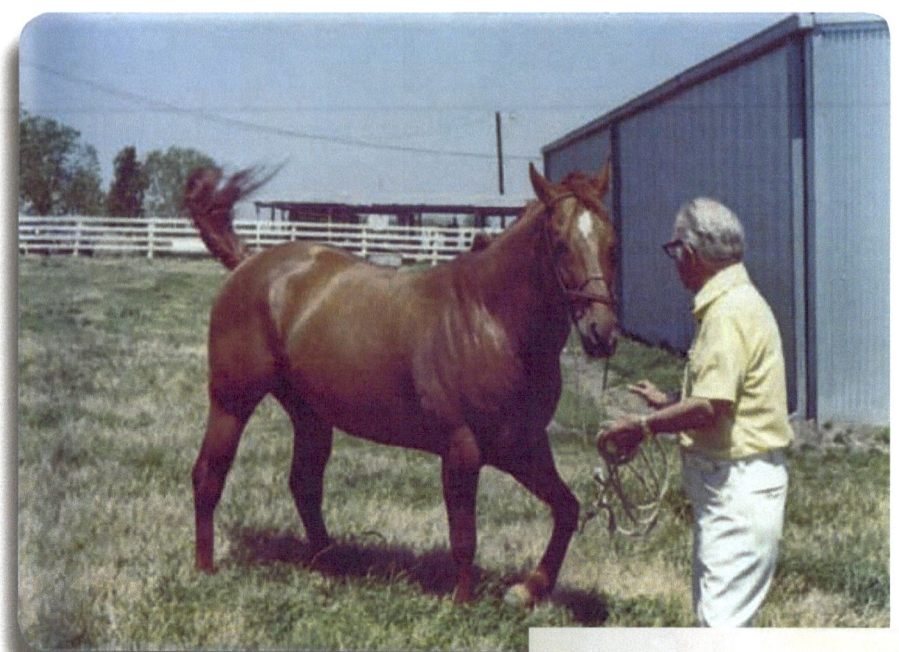

ing else in common.

On that last visit, I found out the Adcocks were running the old store in Culleoka. I stopped by to see Mrs. Adock behind the counter. She greeted me with a warm smile and hugs. I introduced her to my future wife, Lulie.

After dark, we would go down to the bottom and shoot snakes. We also raided the chicken house to shoot rats and mice running along the rafters. These nighttime forays were fully sanctioned by our families. As we got older, we would stay up all night or until the flashlight batteries went dead or our ammunition ran out.

*O*ne night Kent and I stayed up all night and were exhausted. We laid down under the big tree in the yard and when I awoke, I had the worst sunburn in my entire life. Fanny came to the rescue with some kind of poultice made with cow's cream and something else. By the time I got home that weekend, I was shedding skin like an onion.

Many years later, I ran into Kent as East Texas State University. By that time, I was a long-haired Vietnam war protestor. He was in Air Force ROTC. We reminisced about the good times we had together, but we had nothing else in common.

*W*hen I was young, we were constantly going to the farm. We spent some gray weekends there during the winter and many carefree weeks there in summer. Often it was just the four of us: Uncle Laurence, Aunt Fanny, Nancy and me. Red Top Farm and our aunt and uncle were emotional and tangible cornerstones in our lives. Our experiences there had lasting impacts on our lives. I will always appreciate the lessons learned there, though often subtle, which I couldn't appreciate or understand until many decades later.

Jack Melton
Buena Vista, Colorado

Chapter 7

There are so many memories of Red Top Farm from childhood to adulthood. The farm was and remains a special place. Yet it is more.

It is where we became a multi-generational family and we shared our lives and individual perspectives without judgment or recrimination. The farm was a safe place and a fun place for a child to grow up; a haven for the hurts of a child and the sorrows of an adult; and a place to contemplate and to celebrate successes.

Jack and I shared the adventures from the time he could walk until I married the second time in 1979 at age 24. I would not be the person I am without the farm experiences and, of course, Laurence and Fanny. They were the ever-watchful shepherds, the pied pipers and our surrogate grand parents. As we grew older, Mom would take us to Laurence's office at 4:30 p.m. (We were supposed to sit quietly, but I remember wandering through the plant, saying hello to everyone and trying to learn how everything worked.

Then it was into the station wagon to Lakewood to pick up Fanny and all the provisions for the weekend—and off we would go. Everything around the two of them seemed bigger than life, including the farm. Peggy would arrive after work and the party would begin. Marty would come up from Austin with her beau. Bonnye and Hank would come seeking a retreat if you could call numerous kinds of nieces and nephews a quiet place, not to mention the cooking and cleaning. We loved to listen to the stories about earlier times and people we never knew constantly laughing and celebrating family. It all seems like a fairy tale—yet so real.

To city kids the early days were rustic—an outhouse, a root cellar, a wood burning stove for heating and cooking, no air conditioning

and the ever-amazing crank telephone with a multi-party line. We had to stand on a box to use the phone or at least listen to the neighbor's conversation. In the winter, it was freezing inside and out, and in the summer it was sweltering. We loved it all, believing it to be perfect. Still the remodeled kitchen with a real stove, a bathroom, another bedroom and air conditioning made it better for us and especially Fanny.

Over the years there were many different activities, depending on the time of year. Labor Day weekend and the dove hunt were a tradition. Family, the mayor of Dallas, the sheriff, the game warden, farmers, friends, businessmen, and neighbors came to hunt, eat, and drink beer after dusk. Because of the children, Laurence enforced strict rules with guns and drinking.

For a period of time, Laurence kept a fishing boat on Lake Lavon. We fished often. Daddy, Fanny, Laurence, Peggy, Jack and I loved fishing whether on the lake or in the tanks on the farm. Laurence or one of us casting hit Fanny in the back, causing the fishhook to go through her shirt and into her skin. We were dropped at the farm and Laurence took her to the doctor to remove the hook. Besides fishing, Peggy and others waterskied. Once, Peggy fell getting out of the water and went into the boat and broke her arm.

After a busy day, we had cookouts and then waited for dusk and the lightening bugs. Fanny kept fruit jars with holes punched in the lids on the porch. We each grabbed one, catching as many as we could. What we loved most was sleeping on the porch until the winter months. We put the lightening bug jars on the screen rails so we could fall asleep watching them. The beds were lined up side-by-side (8 to 10) with Laurence and Fanny having the taller two beds. We laughed and told ghost stories until Laurence came to bed, and then it was lights out. Even in the summer heat, with fans, we managed to sleep peacefully. At some point, Laurence installed new metal feeders for the hogs. From that point on there was no sleeping late, the hogs started feeding before daylight and the noise traveled the distance across the creek.

Unless there was work to do, we were free to ride the horses, play in the creek, fish, and chase one another through the fields. Laurence had one bull named Shorty. Shorty did not like noisy children running through

his pasture too close to "his cows." More than once, he chased us over, under, and through the fence. There was an old fire bell near the well on the porch. Until the bell rang, or we were hungry or thirsty, we roamed easily without fear. Only at the farm were we permitted such unrestrained freedom.

There was a work ethic as well as enjoyment. If the cattle crossed the creek or the road, we participated in rounding them up. We helped Fanny in the garden and helped Laurence assemble new chicken coops, feed the cattle and livestock and worm the young chicks. I can still feel the bumps of riding in the World War II jeep across the pasture and jumping out to open and close the gates. Laurence loved gadgets. He installed the first rural electric fence in the area. We helped by being guinea pigs for the adjustments necessary to deter the livestock and not hurt us.

When we were young, we came as a family. Later, Daddy would take us so that he could hunt and fish. Mom didn't come until we had air conditioning. As we grew older, Mom would drop us off at the printing company. She and Dad would drive up on Sunday for dinner and to take us home. Fanny and Bonnye prepared the best dinners. We picked the produce, shelled the peas, and shucked the corn. Some Sundays, there were five or six, other times we could hardly find room around the huge round antique table. I also remember the

Germans killing their own as he marched them back to his camp. (He told us there were more than were listed in the newspaper account because so many were killed by Germans firing on their own troops because they surrendered before the shell attack. He described the trenches and being gassed. Even as a child, I knew he was spared for his family and greater reasons to come. To my knowledge, he did not speak of those days again.

pump organ player. The tunes were "Oh Suzanna," "Old Man River"—the music and the times were simple. Someone looking in might see the layers of life displayed weekend after weekend, year after year.

As an example, we heard the stories from other family members about our uncle's experiences during World War I. We often pestered Laurence to tell us the story. One cold Sunday morning before Fanny got up, Uncle Laurence and Jack lit the fire in the iron stove. He said we were old enough to hear the story, but once he finished, we were never to ask him to relive those days. He was on patrol with two or three others when they got behind enemy lines. They found a foxhole some time during the night; he fell asleep and heard his brother, Leo's voice saying, "Keep your head down." He could not remember how long he was asleep, but he awoke to find his comrades shot through the head. He told us about the German soldiers surrendering and the

It is fitting that on my last trip to the farm with Daddy, Jack, Lulie, my fiancée, and his daughter. We had to crawl through the fence of the "little white house" to reach the tank. It was late May and I was hot and tired. I sat down on the bank to fish and promptly received hundreds of chigger bites. It was not the first time, but it was the last.

Aside from the all-around good times, the farm was a loving, safe place to escape the rigors of adult life and to provide freedom from city life for generations of kids. You could be

yourself whether your were seven or seventy. Laurence and Fanny welcomed all with open arms and generosity, Red Top farm bridged the generations and nurtured the meaning of family. We experienced a way of life that was slipping away. I smile when I recall the words, "Let's go to the farm." Every family of every generation shares the same smile when you mention the farm.

Thank you Uncle Laurence and Aunt Fanny.

Nancy Melton
Plano, Texas

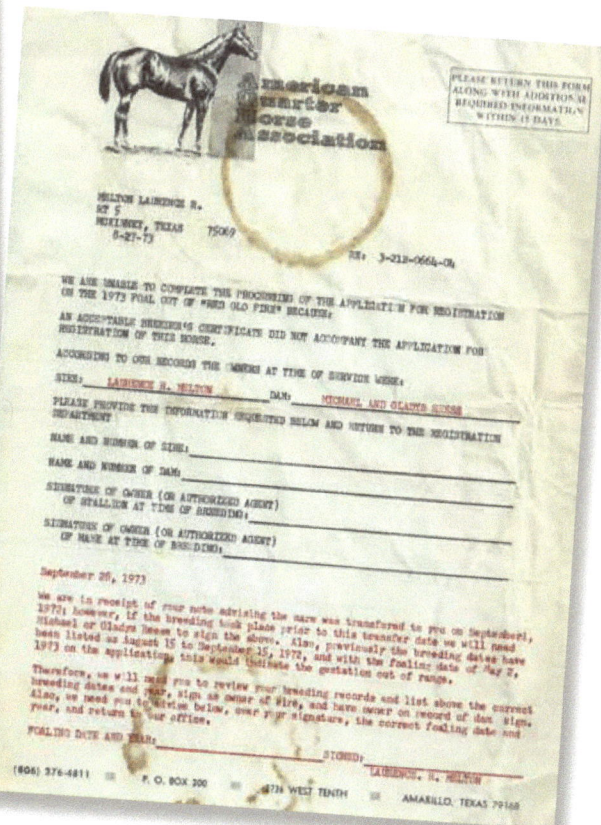

Chapter 8

It is interesting that many of the family had the same
or similar experiences at Red Top, but saw them
in different perspectives and introspection.

*E*ach of us has kept the essence of the experience close to us all through our lives, and the memories are clear to this day.

In the early 1970s, the Corps of Engineers decided to enlarge Lake Lavon. They took several acres of pastureland and raised the level of the lake 25 feet. That gave Red Top Farm lakefront. My father did not develop the lakefront and it made a beautiful view from the main house.

I suppose the best way to remember the farm is the great companionship my parents conveyed to all, especially the young family members. At the farm there was time to just be together and "feel" the love they felt for you. There was riotous fun and excitement, but the best of all was time spent together, shelling peas or sitting together watching the orange and silver streaks of a sunset, or sitting on the bank of a pond—with nothing to do. There was a sense that all this was put together with no practical purpose, except enchantment for a time past and family togetherness.

This enchantment lasted over 40 years. Even when my parents became elderly, there were trips to the farm, not so often, but to "check on things."

Then in 1978, my father Laurence (Lunk) died. The dynamic force behind Red Top Farm was lost to us. The farm was shut up tight and only occasionally did anyone go there for a day's outing. My daughters, Linda, Laura and Robin would spend the day once in a while. Sometime they would spend the night, but it was never the same. My mother and I would

51

go and we both felt sad on the return trip home. During one of these trips back to town, I suggested that we might reopen the house, fix it up and spend some time there that summer. Fanny was all for it. In fact, she immediately she made trips to Home Depot. I was living with her then, separating from my husband and trying to sort out my future. It seemed like a great project for the both of us.

I have never worked so hard as during those springtime months. On our hands and knees, we pulled up the carpet, scraped the old wooden floors and stained them. We discarded all the knick-knacks and kept only the meaningful family heirlooms. Our goal was to make it as authentic as it once was—and we did. We painted the kitchen walls red and bought an antique breadbox and canisters and put out the old Mixmaster, my mother's meat grinder and other old kitchen tools she used to work with so often. Redoing the house was hard work, but fun with my mother beside me. We laughed a lot and drank gallons of lemonade and iced tea. One time that turned into hilarity when we were carrying a heavy hooked rung into the house. We had to put it down and sit on the grass until we calmed down. But. Oh, we were so proud and our family was, too.

That summer was "the way we were," kind of summer. My family had enlarged and they came. Dinners were once again celebrated around the large round oak table. That table had seen so many meals and had been laden with fresh farm produce, enjoyed by dozens of

friends and family. That table and chairs must be 150 years old and has stayed in the family. After enjoying the farm that summer, it was closed for the winter.

The following is something I wrote while the farm was "at rest."

1896 and 1986

It is an old story. We've seen it set to music, tearful drama, and hilarious comedy. It's a story we all relate to—especially if "we all" are Texans. Texans are historically strong individualists. An old settler called it the "Feisty, risk-loving, me-first Texas style." A Texan and his land are measured as one and Texans can be fanatically territorial.

I heard the following story once at the feet of an elderly relative at a family reunion:

The discovery of the cut barbed-wire drove Addie into a rage. She and her sons had worked long days in miserable cold to confine the few head of cattle that were left. It seemed much longer than a year since Matthew had died and left her seven children to farm on their own. Addie was proud of the last year, but times like these made her weary and wondering if she could hold out. She knew that the ranchers, Malone was their name, had trespassed on her farm to run their cattle to market. Addie had never met any of the Malones and they had never stopped to ask permission to cut through the farm. After rounding up her livestock for the fourth time, she was enraged. Addie was determined to prove to everyone, a woman alone and unprotected could not be ignored or run over.

Dressed in her best church clothes and armed with freshly baked berry pies, Addie loaded her wagon with her family and rode it into battle. The Malones lived camp style and were a rough and rowdy bunch of men. A woman's touch to their place was not in evidence. Sweet as sugar, Addie brought the pies out and placed them on the table as gifts. Perplexed, the men began to drool in anticipation. Suddenly, Addie and her children scooped up the pies and began throwing. Pies slammed into the face if each of the ranchers.

Unbelievable, stunned and licking the berries off themselves, they could only listen. Addie declared her determination. They were never, under any circumstances, to trespass on her land without asking. Furthermore, she let them know she kept her rifles loaded and she was "bold to use them." If the Malones asked permission to use a passageway, she would consider it. For many year afterwards, the Malones had special permission to use the south canyon to pass through Addie's land. It became traditional to stop at her farmhouse for a piece of berry pie on the return trip.

Yesterday, the phone rang while I was visiting my mother. Fanny answered. I could hear an indignant response from her as she was told that there were trespassers on her farm. Fanny's farm had been a large part of her life and the farm became a center of our family life for many years. Since my father's death, my mother gradually and painfully let the farm to return to just land and vacant houses and barns.

The neighbor who called said men had driven a fire truck into the barn. "Yes I saw it myself! They were even mixing cement to floor the barn."

Astonished by their nerve, Fanny went right to the coat closet, put on her coat and said to my sister and me, "Let's go take care of them!" We finally persuaded her that there was nothing to be done after dark and it was twenty-five degrees outside as well. Fanny paced the floor into the morning hours and my sister and I feared the conflict awaiting us at dawn.

Fence-cutters, cattle drivers, rustlers, yes, but firemen? Morning brought another phone call, the helpful neighbor. "You won't BELIEVE the front page of the Clarion. There's a picture of three firemen on a fire truck beside YOUR barn. The caption says: VOLUNTEER FIRE DEPARTMENT PROUD OF NEW HOME ON MELTON FARM."

"Well that does it! We're driving out right now."

We followed Fanny out the door like soldiers following General Sam Houston. Our battle cry was, "We're going to fight fire with fire!"

During the drive my mother talked of "taking advantage of a woman alone, "They think because I am old! If they had only asked me," and "Trespassing is despicable."

The farm was bleak looking. Winter was half over and the fields were frozen brown. Patches of fertile black soil had been plowed for early planting. Barren trees were silhouetted against a grey sky. The tenant, a prominent member of the Volunteer Fire Department was nowhere to be found. In fact, we wondered just how a person would report a fire. We walked against the wind to the barn and rolled back the huge door. There it was—backed in, shining and ready to meet an emergency. The proud Engine #11! Five hooks held five heavy coats. Above the coats were five hats, emblems glistening. Beneath were five pairs of boots lined up in precise order. A banner proclaimed: "Our Community Volunteers." Cement had indeed been poured and a rickety table and five chairs had been moved in.

Fanny was beside herself, exclaiming in very breath, "the nerve." It doesn't matter if they have improved things, they are still trespassers."

We stopped at the country store down the road where the fire chief works. He wasn't there, but as if "to add fuel to the fire." Fanny pointed out a poster advertising raffle tickets could be bought to aid the fire department. The woman behind the counter told Fanny that if she bought a ticket, she could possibly win a smoked turkey or a ham. "The department wants to purchase an equipment truck," she said.

"Oh no," Fanny gasped.

We encouraged Fanny to the car and left to devise a response.

On the drive back to town Fanny said to us, "well, I think it is a good thing and I really should be helpful."

A letter was composed and Fanny made it clear who was in charge of the farm, but she had thought back. She knew an era had ended. I am certain I see traces of the past in this episode and equally certain that Fanny is the pie-throwing kind.

So the farm stood idle and the years saw it return to the state it was when I first saw it. There were only a few signs of the time out there. The iron bridge over the gully was there; also part of the rail fence, the replica of an old red barn, and the tin barrel where we burned trash. I am reminded that early one Sunday morning, my mother received a call from a Collin County sheriff. The farm had been burglarized. We rushed there to find all the antiques gone, pictures taken, quilted bed coverings, the old organ, even the food out of the pantry. It was a distressing sight, but my mother just locked the door and walked to the car. She was so practical. Nothing could bring it all back.

I traveled to all the flea markets in North Texas, hoping to recover something from the farm. I never found anything.

Two years passed. Another phone call came in to inform my mother that vandals had set fire to the house and it was a charred ruin—and it was. Only a shell remained.

Considering the story of Red Top Farm, and all the memories, I find myself wondering if the next generations will miss the greatest way to learn how rewarding life can be is through simplicity. The virtue of hospitality and sociability were learned at the farm. Lessons were taught by example and learned by completing a task successfully. Everyday, mundane things can be adventurous and create an appreciation of nature. Red Top Farm showed us the importance of a cohesive supportive system in work and play.

When Fanny passed away in 2001, my sister Peggy and I decided to sell. Now it has become a "Country Bed and Breakfast." It is run by a young couple, who want to experience a simple way of life.